Contents

Confetti 2

Azure 26

Bauble 5

Twilight 29

Filigree 8

Copper 32

Carbon 11

Cochineal 35

Gossamer 14

Essential Materials 38
Other Equipment 39
Knitting Techniques 40
Crochet Techniques 42
How to French Knit 44
How to Plait 44
Finishing Off 45
Troubleshooting 47
Conversions 48

Clementine 17

Cobalt 20

Cluster 23

Introduction

Be the envy of your friends by creating unique and beautiful wire jewelry in myriad colors and custom made to suit any occasion. Using the simplest of knitting, French knitting, crocheting, and twisting techniques, you can make fabulous bracelets, necklaces, and earrings to match any outfit.

All the projects are easy to make, and each is accompanied by clear instructions to guide you through the process. You can follow them to the letter or use them as a basis for your own creations. The projects are so simple that most can be made in just one evening. A handy techniques section explains all the basic skills needed, making these projects suitable for experienced jewelry makers and novices alike.

Confetti

An easy-to-knit necklace, this can be made with large or small beads. Both produce stunning results. Bracelets and earrings can be made to match.

YOU WILL NEED

- 22yd (20m) of 0.315mm (AWG 28:SWG 30) wire
- 2.25mm (US-1:UK13) knitting needles
- Selection of beads and sequins in various sizes
- Crimp beads
- Fastening of your choice

FOR A PROFESSIONAL FINISH...

When arranging your beads, use a tape measure for guidance. Place bigger feature beads every 4in (10cm) and balance your other beads along the length. Play with the colors until you are happy with the result.

Don't place beads on each row as you will run out of beads and the necklace will be uncomfortable to wear. Place your beads to fill gaps in the previous row. So, if you place beads on stitches 1, 3, and 5, on the next beading row put them on stitches 2, 4, and 6.

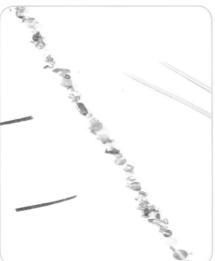
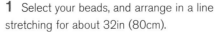

1 Select your beads, and arrange in a line stretching for about 32in (80cm).

2 Unwind about 6ft (1.8m) of wire from the reel and re-secure with the elastic band. Thread on your beads, mixing sizes and shapes.

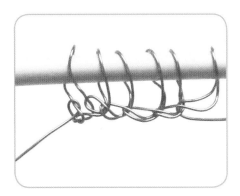

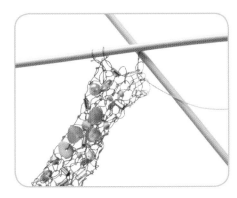

3 Cast on 6 stitches, leaving a 4in (10cm) tail.

4 Knit Row 1. Knit Row 2, placing three or four beads across the row.

5 Repeat, adding beads on the even-numbered rows, until you have the required length of about 20in (50cm).

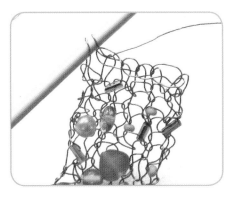

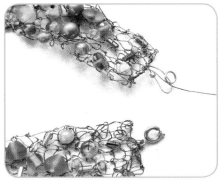

6 To finish, bind off, leaving a 4in (10cm) tail. Place the necklace on a flat surface and ease into a curved shape using the palms of your hands.

7 Wrap the tail along the edge to the center, neatening as you go. Use it to attach one half of the fastening. Slip a crimp bead on the wire before looping it between the fixing of the fastening and the center of the edge. Tuck the end of the wire under the crimp bead and squeeze to secure. Cut off any surplus wire. Repeat for the other end.

VARIATIONS YOU CAN TRY...

Try making your necklace wider by casting on eight stitches instead of six, or make it narrower by using only four stitches. You can get quite a different look by beading in the center of the necklace only; alternatively, you could place a few larger beads here, making the rest of the necklace wire-only.

For a fun alternative, make a narrow necklace using pink wire and ⅝in (14mm) buttons—you'll need about 40 of them; place the buttons on every fourth row.

Bauble

This is a pretty and fragile-looking necklace with a lovely looped edge. Pearl beads give it a classic feel, but the delicate wirework gives it a fresh twist. It is knitted on fine wire, using double-pointed needles.

FOR A PROFESSIONAL FINISH...

Be careful not to catch the wire on the bead below as you are beading, otherwise you will have a large loop when you've finished. If this does happen, twist the loop into the necklace to hide it.

Work a couple of unbeaded rows at the beginning and end of the necklace to make attaching the fastening easier.

The loop of wire always falls on the same side of the work. If you are not beading, then this should be the wrong side of the necklace.

YOU WILL NEED

- 22yd (20m) of 0.25mm (AWG 30:SWG 33) wire
- 2.25mm (US-1:UK13) double-pointed knitting needles
- About 125 beads, approximately ¼in (6mm) in size
- Fastening of your choice

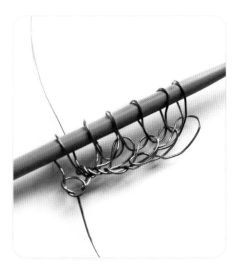

1 Thread the beads on the wire. I used 125 x ¼in (6mm) beads to make a necklace 18in (45cm) long.

2 Cast on 6 stitches. Then work 1 row. Knit every stitch—don't slip the first one.

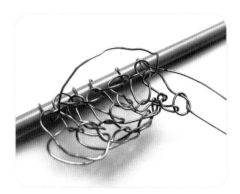 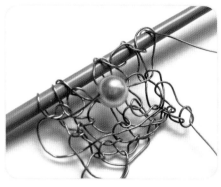 

3 Slide the work up to the top of the needle. Work another row. There will be a loop of wire across the work; don't pull this loop tightly across the work as this will stop it from lying flat.

4 Slide the work up to the top of the needle again. Bring up a bead and knit 1 row. (The bead sits on the loop of wire.)

5 Repeat for required length of beading on every row, remembering to slide the work each time. Give a gentle tug after each row to shape the necklace as you go.

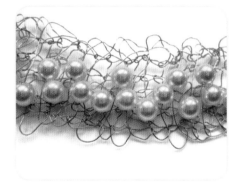 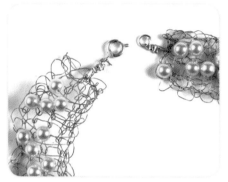

6 Bind off with beaded side facing you. When finished, tease out the loops at the edge of the work with one of the needles.

7 Ease the necklace into shape by gently pulling it. Then attach the fastening.

VARIATIONS YOU CAN TRY...

This is a very versatile project that works equally well for a narrower necklace (four stitches). It looks good with both random and regular beading, or you can even make an unbeaded version.

Try making the necklace with longer beads, which sit well on the wire. You could also try weaving ⅝in (1.5cm) wide ribbon through the loops—use a large-eyed needle to thread the ribbon through.

For a pair of matching earrings, cast on three stitches and work four beaded rows. Bind off and attach the posts.

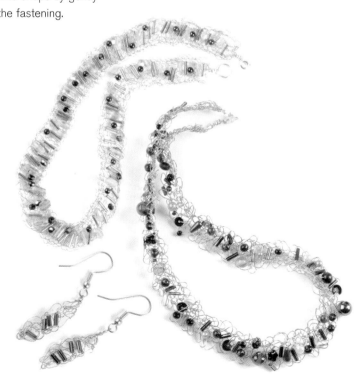

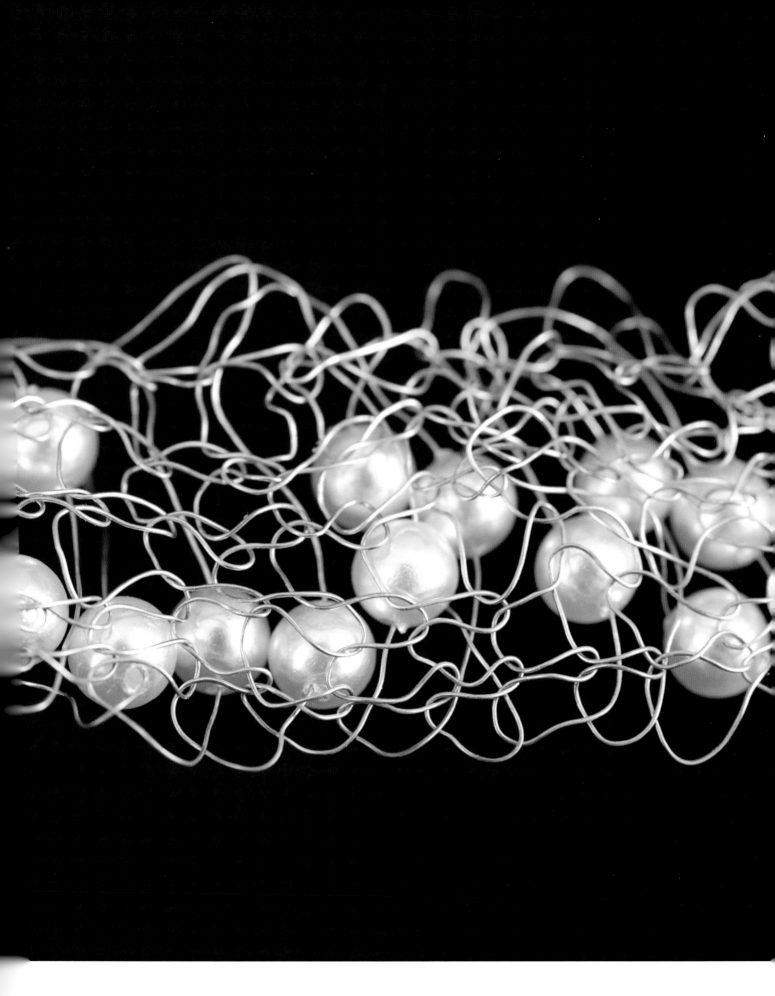

Filigree

A fragile-looking necklace that looks equally good
as a choker or short chain. Enhanced with tiny Swarovski
beads that sparkle beautifully, this pretty necklace
is a winner for the evening.

YOU WILL NEED

- 22yd (20m) of 0.2mm
  (AWG 32:SWG 36) wire
- 2.25mm (US-1:UK13)
  knitting needles
- About 50 Swarovski beads
- Magnetic or screw fastening

FOR A PROFESSIONAL FINISH...

Don't worry if the work looks uneven, particularly at the beginning. As you progress you will see the lacy effect begin to emerge.

After binding off the finished work, hold it in your right hand and the bead in your left. Twist each bead three times clockwise to fix the bead in position. Work along the necklace for each bead, being careful not to over twist.

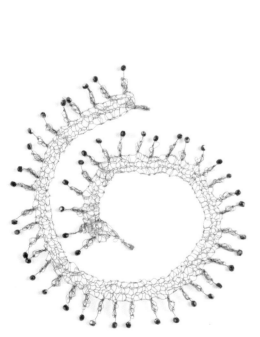

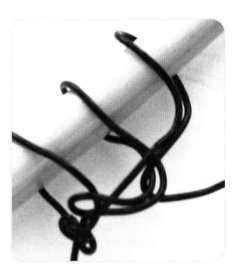

1 Thread the beads onto the wire. The fine wire used means this necklace is quite light.

2 Cast on 3 stitches.

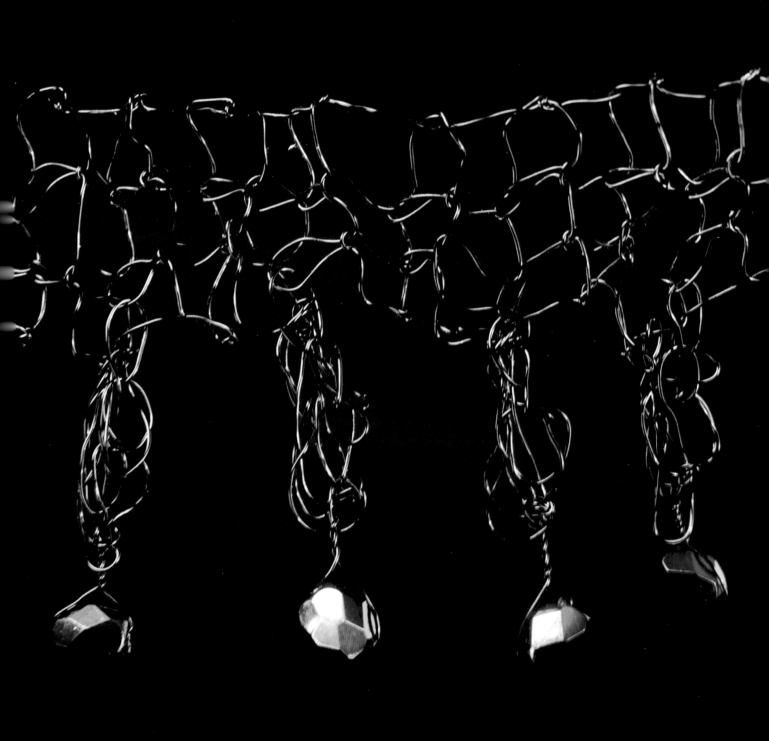

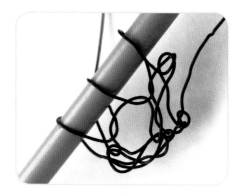

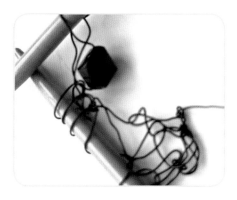

3 Knit 3 rows. Work evenly—if you work too tightly, you won't get the delicate effect.

4 Row 4: Cast on 4 stitches (7 stitches).

5 Row 5: Bead on the first stitch.

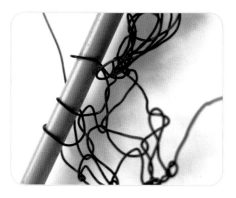

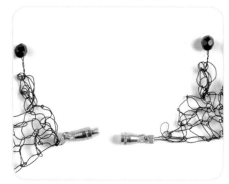

6 Bind off 4 stitches and knit the remaining 3 stitches. Give the bead a tug as you bind off each stitch to keep them even.

7 Knit 3 rows. Repeat from step 4 until you reach the required length.

8 Work 2 rows, then bind off. Attach the fastening. Use a magnetic or screw fastening, which is easy to secure.

VARIATIONS YOU CAN TRY...

It's easy to make a wider or narrower collar by casting on more or fewer stitches at the start.

Earrings can be fun. To make short earrings, cast on 12 stitches, bead, bind off six stitches. Cast on six stitches, bead, then bind off. Alternatively, try casting on and binding off, randomly beading as you please. Make the strands at the top slightly longer so you get more of a "branch" effect. The wire is light so these earrings won't be heavy to wear.

Carbon

Using a French-knitting bobbin, you can produce an easy and unusual necklace. It is also readily adjusted for length.

FOR A PROFESSIONAL FINISH...

Make sure that the beads are small enough to fit through the center of the bobbin. The beads sit inside the wire and can be as close together as you wish.

You can just pop the beads down the center of the work, but threading them on the wire ensures that they stay in place and can't escape through the mesh.

YOU WILL NEED
- 22yd (20m) of 0.315mm (AWG 28:SWG 30) wire
- Four-pin French-knitting bobbin
- Cable needle
- About 70 assorted small beads
- Fastening of your choice

1 Thread the beads onto the wire. Make a slip knot and put the loop over one of the bobbin pins.

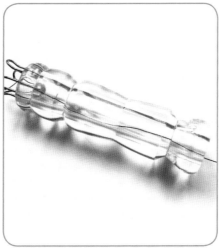

2 Pass the wire tail down the center of the bobbin so that it can be pulled from the bottom. This will help tension the work.

3 Start knitting and work one complete round. The first stitch can be difficult to lift over; keep the slip knot loose to make this easier.

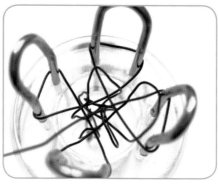

4 Work two more complete rounds, working in a clockwise direction.

5 Thread the first bead, holding it down the center of the bobbin.

6 Continue knitting until you have the length you want, placing the beads as required.

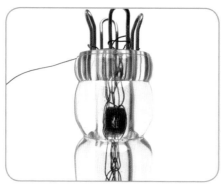

7 Finish off by sliding the four loops off the pins, and passing the working end of the wire through the loops. Pull the working end firmly to gather the ends together.

8 Attach the fastening.

VARIATIONS YOU CAN TRY...

If you want to make a necklace using larger beads, use an eight-pin bobbin, which should have a larger center hole.

If you are using fine wire, which can be a bit limp and not hold its shape, make three strands and twist together. Or, layer the strands, one above the other.

A bracelet makes a great first project; all you need to do is adjust the length.

Gossamer

A beautiful, delicate necklace that is easy to adjust
for length and can be worked in a variety of colors
to match any outfit. It is very attractive unbeaded,
or you can add sparkly Swarovski beads.

YOU WILL NEED

- 22yd (20m) of 0.2mm
  (AWG 32:SWG 36) wire,
  3 lengths in 3 toning colors
- Four-pin French-knitting bobbin
- Cable needle
- Fastening of your choice

FOR A PROFESSIONAL FINISH...

Fine wire works best for this project, and holds its shape well when plaited.

If necessary, pinch the necklace between your thumb and forefinger to flatten and
ease into shape.

Twisting the loose ends together will prevent the plait from undoing, but take care
not to over twist them.

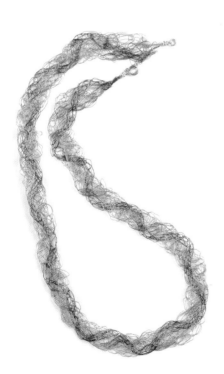

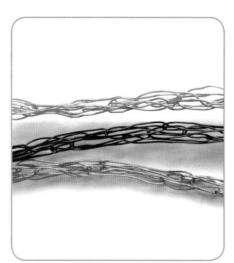

1 Cast on four loops, and then work
the required length of necklace plus 4in
(10cm). Finish off the end. Do this three
times, using wire of the same weight.

2 The wire will appear rather thin because
you will have tugged it through the bobbin
as you worked. To rectify this, take each
chain in turn, hold it between your thumbs
and index fingers, and gently pull it to make
it wider. Alternatively, use a cable needle to
tease the chain apart.

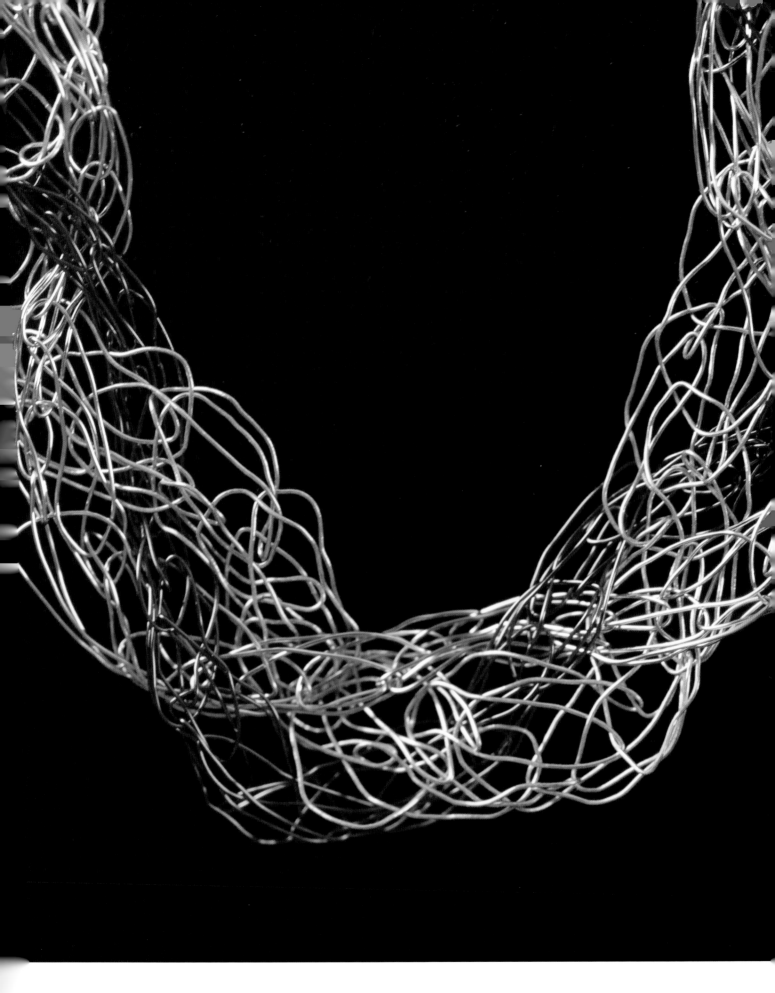

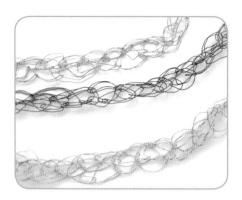

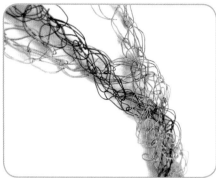

3 You should find that the chain flattens and makes a band about ½in (1cm) wide. Repeat for all three.

4 Now twist the three ends together. Plait the strands, easing them into shape as you go. Don't pull tightly or the shape of the necklace will distort.

5 Shape the necklace on a flat surface when the plaiting is finished and twist the ends together.

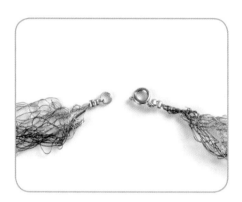

6 Attach the fastening.

VARIATIONS YOU CAN TRY…

You can use a medium wire, for a firmer, more defined necklace or a choker. Try making two of the three plaits the same color. Or be ambitious and make a five-strand plait.

For a beaded necklace, choose small sparkly beads and a piece of matching wire. Attach the end of the wire close to the fastening and weave it through the plaited work for about ¼in (6mm). Add a bead and continue weaving, making sure that the beads sit on the surface of the necklace. Locate the beads as frequently as you wish, making sure that the weaving wire is hidden well in the plait.

Bracelets and earrings are easy to make, using shorter plaits. Be sure that you don't make the earrings too wide when you are teasing them into shape.

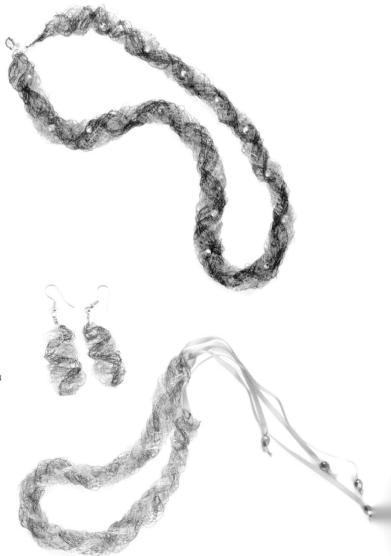

Clementine

An unusual necklace that is worked on two pins for a delicate and light effect. Weaving a fine ribbon through the wire finishes off your necklace—adding a large central bead gives it a different dimension altogether.

FOR A PROFESSIONAL FINISH...

The chain will be narrow at first because you will have tugged it through the bobbin. Tease it out carefully. You can use your fingers, but it might make them feel a bit sore; you may prefer to use the point of a cable needle instead.

Make sure there are no sharp ends of wire to scratch the skin. Bend them carefully back into the work with pliers.

YOU WILL NEED

- 22yd (20m) of 0.315mm (AWG 28:SWG 30) wire
- Four-pin French-knitting bobbin
- Cable needle
- Length of ribbon of desired length
- Selection of beads, if required
- Magnetic or twist fastening

1 Make a slip knot, put the loop over one of the bobbin pins, and pass the tail down the center of the bobbin.

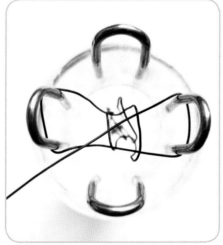

2 Work on two opposite pins to make a chain.

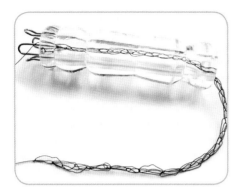

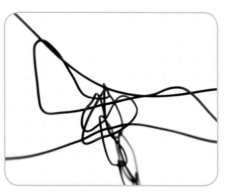

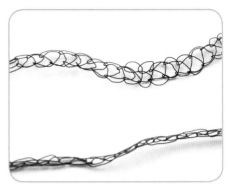

3 Continue working until the chain is 1¼in (3cm) longer than the finished length that you require.

4 Finish off the loops, and remove from the bobbin.

5 On a soft surface—such as a fabric table mat—tease out the wire into a looped, open chain.

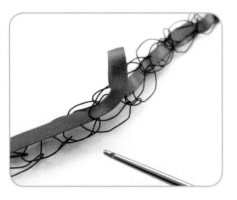

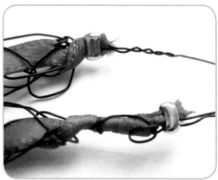

6 Using the point of the cable needle, thread a ribbon through the center of the wire, keeping it as flat as possible.

7 Taper the end of the ribbon, and pass it through a larger crimp bead before threading through the wire. Trim the ribbon off close to the first crimp bead. Attach the fastenings.

8 Attach the beads after you have finished making the necklace. As this necklace is lightweight, the beads should be, too. Use a separate piece of wire and weave the end through the work, one bead at a time. Place the beads centrally for best effect.

VARIATIONS YOU CAN TRY...

Using different colored ribbon and beads will give your necklace a quite different look. You could use two pieces of ribbon of different colors, and perhaps attach a central drop as well. For a lacy effect, try using a lighter wire on a larger bobbin.

Try making earrings to match. Count the rounds very carefully so they both finish up the same length.

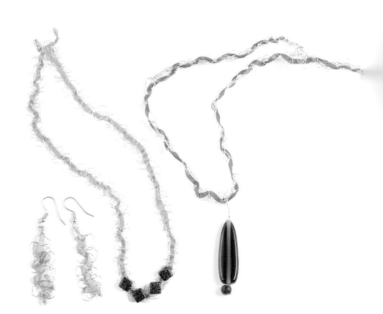

Cobalt

This is a simple crocheted necklace that can easily be adjusted for a variety of lengths. It can also be made up of single or multiple strands.

YOU WILL NEED

- 22yd (20m) of 0.25mm (AWG 30:SWG 33) wire
- 2.75mm (USC-2:UK12) crochet hook
- Selection of beads
- Fastening of your choice

FOR A PROFESSIONAL FINISH...

Try working a few chain stitches on a scrap piece of wire to practise getting the perfect tension. Don't pull the wire too tightly.

It is better to work this necklace in one sitting as the tension will be more even and the beads will sit better on the chain.

Try not to work more chain than is needed; the wire is likely to snap if you try to undo your stitches, and the kinks are difficult to remove.

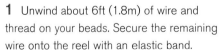

1 Unwind about 6ft (1.8m) of wire and thread on your beads. Secure the remaining wire onto the reel with an elastic band.

2 Make a slip knot in the wire.

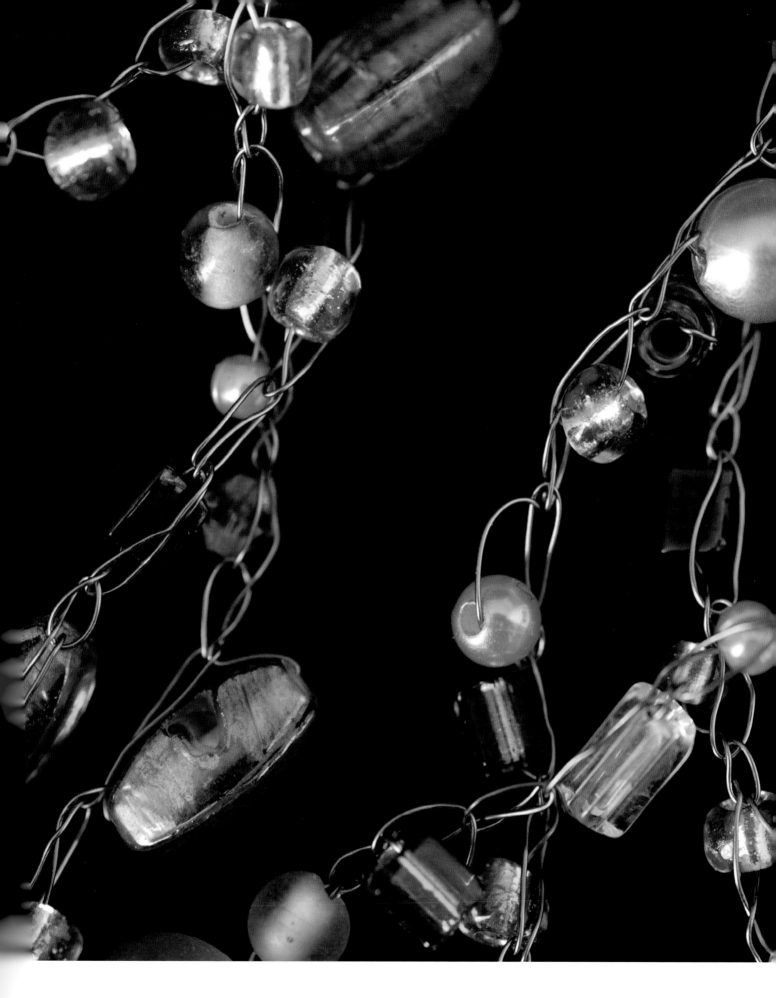

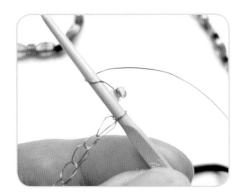

3 Begin crocheting and work about 6 chain.

4 Bead on alternate chain stitches until you reach the required length; about 28in (70cm) is a good length. If you are using larger beads, place them further apart.

5 Finish with 6 chain to match the beginning of the necklace.

6 Cut the wire and pass it through the last chain to secure. Attach a fastening if you are making a single chain.

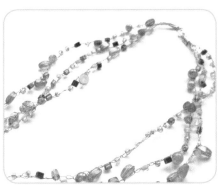

7 If you want to make a necklace with several strands, repeat the process two or three times more, making each chain shorter by 3in (7.5cm). Lay the strands out flat and ease out any kinks. Bring the ends together and pass through one crimp bead. Adjust and squeeze crimp to hold the ends; this makes attaching a fastening much easier to do.

VARIATIONS YOU CAN TRY...

Work more than one chain in different colors, adjusting the length of strands so that they sit nicely on your neck. Place heavier beads at the center of the necklace for a more dramatic effect, or add a feature bead at the center. You could also try randomly placing assorted beads and working several chains. Experiment with hooks; the larger the hook that you use, the "loopier" the chain.

For earrings, make a short-beaded chain joined in a loop, and attach them to the ear wire with crimp beads.

Cluster

A beautiful chunky necklace, which uses toning beads to good effect on three chains. This method works particularly well for bracelets, too.

FOR A PROFESSIONAL FINISH...

Make the bead mixture really random by putting the beads in a dish and giving them a good stir. Select your beads by dipping into the dish without looking.

The chain needs to be about 28in (70cm) for a finished necklace length of 23in (60cm). Adjust accordingly if you want a shorter necklace.

If the necklace is too long when you have finished, simply scrunch it up. Push the chains together and make a denser necklace.

YOU WILL NEED

- 22yd (20m) of 0.315mm (AWG 28:SWG 30) wire
- 3mm (USD-3:UK10) crochet hook
- Selection of beads
- Fastening of your choice

1 Thread the beads onto the wire (you need plenty of them as you are going to make three strands). Make a slip loop, then crochet 2 chain.

2 Bead, crochet 1 chain, bead, crochet 1 chain. Repeat to end.

3 Make the strand the finished necklace length plus 4in (10cm). Finish by passing the tail through the last chain loop.

4 Repeat two more times. Then take the three crochet strands and twist together the ends of wire.

5 Fix the twisted wires to a drawer handle or something secure and begin to plait. Overlap the strands, easing the beads into place so that they sit nicely without gaps. The plait doesn't need to be tight so don't pull too much.

6 Finish the ends by twisting them together, and then attach the fastenings.

VARIATIONS YOU CAN TRY…

This is a great necklace for using up any odd beads, and a toning mixture of variously sized beads works really well. Try alternating a gold-colored spacer bead between the colored beads, for an evening necklace, or try smaller beads for a lighter effect.

For an even chunkier necklace, make five strands and plait them together. Make a shorter length for a matching bracelet, but be sure to use a secure fastening since this design can be quite heavy.

Azure

An easy-to-make necklace featuring a large central bead to make a dramatic impact. It works equally well for daytime or night-time, depending on the beads that you use. Larger ones are best.

YOU WILL NEED

- 22yd (20m) of 0.315mm (AWG 28:SWG 30) wire
- 3.25mm (USD-3:UK10) crochet hook
- Selection of beads
- Fastening of your choice

FOR A PROFESSIONAL FINISH...

Where you have a central bead, work out the length of the first side accordingly; put in extra chain stitches if needed so that the bead sits in the center. Match the second side to the first.

A gentle tug to one side or the other will even out the length of the necklace if it is uneven.

1 Before threading the beads, plan out your necklace on the table to ensure that each side matches. Thread the beads onto the wire.

2 Make a slip loop and work 4 chain.

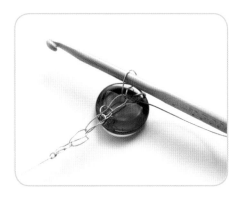  

3 Bring up the first bead and crochet a chain stitch to hold it in place. This may have to be a slightly larger stitch, depending on the size of the bead used. Don't let it get too big as the bead will not stay in place.

4 Work 3 chain and then work the next bead.

5 Repeat for the remainder of the beads. The chain stitches need to be worked evenly for the best results.

6 As you have only a single strand of wire at the finishing end, introduce another doubled piece to make it stronger before attaching the fastening.

VARIATIONS YOU CAN TRY…

Wooden beads look good, but you'll need a few heavier beads at the front to get the chain to sit nicely.

For a real statement, try using a huge central bead instead. You can play with different shapes with this necklace: you might like round beads on the chain with a large square bead as the central drop.

Try choosing a wire color that provides a good contrast to the color of the beads for a really striking effect.

Twilight

This pretty necklace is very easy to make: you simply use twisting to hold the beads in place. It can be a single strand or a layered necklace and is very quick to do.

FOR A PROFESSIONAL FINISH...

Do not over twist as there is a risk of snapping the wire. Four or five twists between each bead should be enough and will give a gap of about ½in (1cm). It is best to use fine wire for this project since thicker wire can be a bit rigid.

Watch that you don't untwist a previous bead as you are working the next one; keep checking as you go along. When you reach the end, work back along the necklace putting any twists that have come out back in place.

YOU WILL NEED
- 2 x 22yd (20m) lengths of 0.2mm (AWG 32:SWG 36) wire in contrasting colors
- About 60 small beads
- A few larger central beads
- Fastening of your choice
- Crimp beads

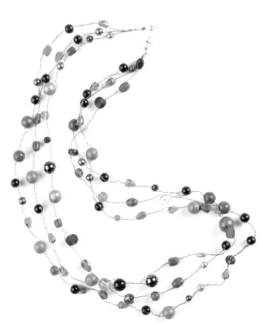

1 Thread the beads onto one of the lengths of wire.

2 Twist and then tie the ends of the wire together. Holding some beads in your right hand, twist the two wires together, trapping a bead in place. Always twist in the same direction and ensure that the wire is twisting between each bead and that you are not just spinning the bead around.

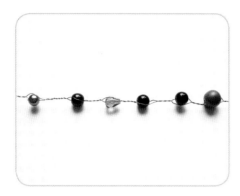

3 Continue along the wire, spacing the beads evenly as you go.

4 When you have sufficient length of necklace, cut the wire ends, twist, and then tie a knot.

5 If you want to make a layered necklace, work more strands of different lengths.

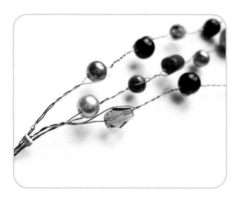

6 Use crimp beads to secure the strands together before attaching a fastening.

VARIATIONS YOU CAN TRY...

This versatile necklace can also be made as a single strand. You can use round or irregularly shaped beads, depending on the effect that you want. You could add a large central bead, flanked by two smaller ones, for dramatic effect.

The piece can be made as a long continuous strand; simply join the ends without a fastening and then wear as a necklace or bracelet.

Copper

This is an easy but effective necklace. It is made with three strands of wire, which are first beaded and then twisted and knotted in place.

YOU WILL NEED

- 3 x 22yd (20m) lengths of 0.2mm (AWG 32:SWG 36) fine wire, in toning colors
- 150 assorted beads, about ⅜in (8mm) in size
- Fastening of your choice

FOR A PROFESSIONAL FINISH...

Make the bead clusters different by varying the number of beads and their position.

The wire in the cluster doesn't need to be too tight: allowing the beads to chink against each other adds to the effect.

Don't tighten the knot until you are happy with its position and have made sure that the three wires are together. Wrap the knot around a finger to fix the wire loop.

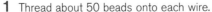

1 Thread about 50 beads onto each wire.

2 Bring the three loose wire ends together and knot them. Bring up some beads from each wire to the knotted end.

3 Cluster the beads so they sit nicely and twist the wire behind them. Don't over twist or it will snap. Make a knot, using all three strands of wire, after the twist.

4 Repeat for the next cluster, twisting and then knotting to hold the beads in place. Try to make the length of twist and the position of the knot the same between each cluster. About five twists should be enough.

5 Continue for the required length, then tie a final knot.

6 Attach the fastening.

VARIATIONS YOU CAN TRY...

Using wire and beads of contrasting colors creates a fun-looking and striking necklace. Try making the central clusters noticeably bigger for an interesting effect; you could also use different center beads.

You can make a matching bracelet using the same basic method, but you will need to position the clusters closer together than for the necklace.

Cochineal

This unusual necklace is quick and easy to make yet has a dramatic impact. A simple twisting technique is all you need to make this attractive design.

FOR A PROFESSIONAL FINISH...

Check that the central bead will fit. Push the knitting needle you intend to wrap around through the hole in the bead; it should fit loosely.

If the hole in the bead is too small, don't worry. Use the central support wire to attach the bead where you want it. Bring it out through the coil in the right place, go back through the bead, then return inside the coil.

If the coil is too long, simply push it up the support wire before crimping. Avoid stretching the coil as it will lose its shape.

> ### YOU WILL NEED
> - 2 x 22yd (20m) lengths of 0.315mm (AWG 28: SWG 30) wire
> - 3.25mm (US-3:UK10) knitting needle
> - 6 crimp beads
> - Fastening of your choice

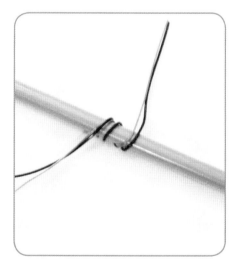

1 Hold the ends of the wire together and begin twisting tightly around the knitting needle. When twisting, turn the needle not the reels as this gives you better control.

2 Push the wire together as you work, ensuring that there are no overlapping twists. Avoid creating kinks in the wire as they will show.

 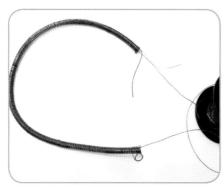 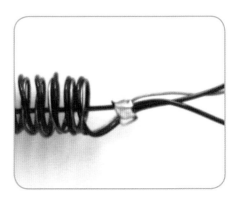

3 Continue with this method until the needle is covered with compacted twists.

4 Slide the work off the needle. Cut the reel ends of the wire. With a strand of wire from one of the reels, push it along the center of the coil.

5 When the wire emerges at each end of the coil, use a crimp bead to secure the wires together. Check the necklace's length and adjust if necessary before you cut the reel end off. The necklace can be shortened by pushing the coils closer together.

 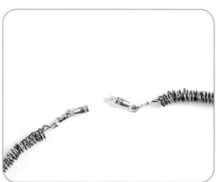

6 Feed a large holed bead along the coil.

7 Attach the fastenings.

VARIATIONS YOU CAN TRY...

Be brave with colors and experiment with different combinations on little test pieces. You can use three colors rather than just two; you can use a lighter wire if you are using three colors.

You can make a necklace with layers of coils. Make sure the central beads fit together well.

For earrings, use a thinner needle and leave a ¾in (2cm) tail of wire for finishing. Make 2¾in (7cm) of compacted coil. Bend the finishing wire at 90 degrees to the coil. Feed the ends through a crimp bead to secure and attach fastenings. Earrings don't need a support wire but a bracelet does.

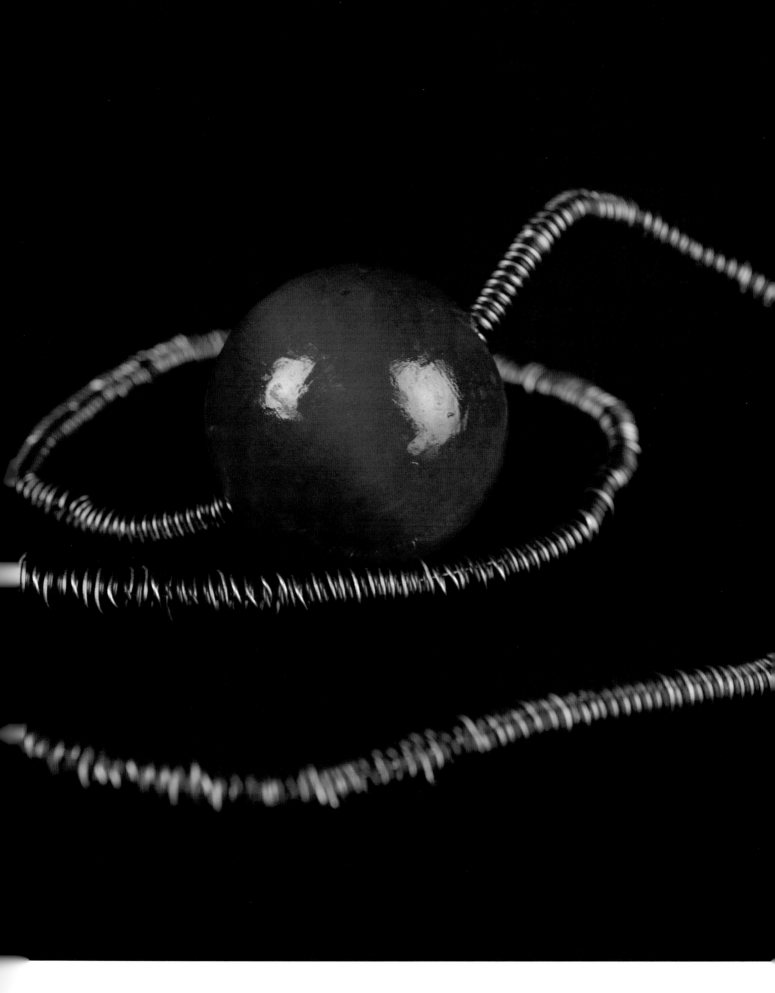

Essential Materials

Wire

The wire needs to be soft enough to bend sufficiently yet strong enough to support the weight of beads that you use.

The projects in this book have all been done in craft wire, which is copper wire with a colored coating. It comes in a beautiful range of colors, and is readily available and inexpensive. The wire also comes in a variety of gauges. For the projects in this booklet I have used fine 0.2mm (AWG 32:SWG 36) wire, a slightly heavier 0.25mm (AWG 30:SWG 33) wire, or a medium wire that is 0.315mm (AWG 28:SWG 30). Anything much heavier becomes difficult to work with and too hard on the fingers.

Wire can be purchased in hanks or on a reel. Hanks need to be rewound carefully on to a spare cotton reel. Secure with an elastic band.

Beads

There is a huge choice of beads available. Glass beads work well—they have a natural "weight," which means they will sit well on the neck. Avoid foiled beads since they can be rubbed by the wire and lose their shine. Gemstones have a lovely random nature and work very well in some of the projects. They can be more expensive than glass beads but are often worth the price.

Wooden beads are a good choice, particularly big chunky ones. Again the natural colors are very attractive.

Some of the projects call for small bead, such as seed beads and long, thin glass beads. Swarovski beads add a lovely sparkle to your work. Look for the ones with AB in the description as these beads have a beautiful iridescent luster.

Metal, ceramic, sequins, gemstone, plastic, pearls and Pandora beads can all be used in wire jewelry. Remember that the beads you use must match the weight of the wire.

Some suppliers offer larger bags of beads (35oz or 1kg), containing a random mixture. These bags are often great value, and offer a good mix of beads to get you started.

Findings

Findings is the name given to all the fastenings and fittings used in jewelry making. The projects in this booklet call for only a few findings; these are readily available, often from bead suppliers.

Clasps Lobster clasps, round clasps, and magnetic or screw fasteners can all be used. A split ring (which looks like a double ring of wire, or a key ring) or a special clasp is used with lobster and round clasps. The screw and magnetic clasps are best used only with lighter-weight pieces; they are not strong enough for heavy beaded necklaces. Avoid jumprings since the wire can escape through the gap if it is not securely fitted. These fastenings are all available in both gold and silver colors, and it is useful to have both of these. Check the measurements, and then match the weight of the necklace to the size of clasp.

Crimp beads These are used to secure the wire when you are attaching fastenings. Usually available in gold, silver, and bronze, they come in different sizes. You are likely to use the smaller sizes more often. They take four strands of wire, while the larger ones can be used with ribbon, too.

Needles and hooks

Each of the projects suggests a needle or hook size to use. These sizes are given as a guide only; by experimenting with different needle or hook sizes, you can produce quite different finished results.

Wire can be hard on fine knitting needles and they tend to bend in use. Most of the knitted projects work best with short needles that range in size from 2.25mm (USB-1:UK13) to 3.25mm (USB-3:UK10). Any larger and the work becomes more open and flexible. It is best if you can reserve specific needles and hooks for your jewelry making.

French-knitting bobbins

These can be found in toy shops and online. Look for the ones that have a looped pin at the top rather than the nail type. Clear plastic bobbins are best since they enable you to see your work as it progresses. French-knitting bobbins usually come with four pins but three-, six-, and eight-pin ones are also available. Some come with a changeable head, giving you more flexibility. You will need a pointed metal tool to lift the wire over the pins. If the bobbin doesn't come with one, then a cable needle (a short, double-pointed needle) will do the job.

Other tools

You will need a pair of pliers; these should be small so you can be accurate in use. Pointed ones are the most useful, and lightweight ones are more comfortable to hold. You do not need wire-cutters; you can use an old pair of scissors to cut the wire. Reserve some specially for jewelry making since they will be spoilt for paper cutting.

Other Equipment

Storage crate

A large, lidded storage crate is very useful for putting bits and pieces away neatly and making your projects much more portable.

Plastic tubs

Translucent food containers are excellent for storing your beads. Avoid compartment boxes—they are too small. Square boxes are best since these pack away neatly in a large crate.

Plastic bags

Use clear zipped bags for storing beads or to keep wire in to stop it unraveling. Small sizes are available online.

Microwave bacon trays

These inexpensive ridged trays are ideal for bead sorting and organizing. The ridges allow you to arrange the beads in rows and see what you've got.

Soft table mat

Working on a fabric table mat will protect your work surface from pointed tools such as a cable needle. It will also help to prevent your beads from rolling around, especially if you use one that has got ridges in the weave.

Ruler and tape measure

A tape measure for checking lengths can save a lot of wasted effort. Undoing work is difficult and leaves kinks in the wire, which can cause the wire to break.

Cotton reels and elastic bands

Empty cotton reels are ideal for winding up hanks of wire (you should never try working straight from the hank as it is guaranteed to knot and tangle). Secure the wrapped wire with an elastic band, then place the cotton reel in a small zipped bag to stop it from unwrapping.

Good light

This is essential to prevent eye strain. It is best to work in daylight, since then you will be able to see the true colors of the beads you are using. Try to look up from your work regularly and refocus on distant objects to give your eyes a rest.

Knitting Techniques

MAKING A SLIP KNOT

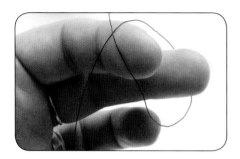 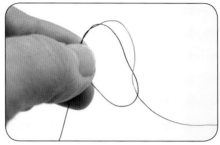 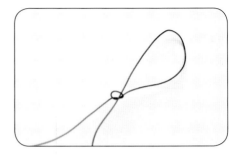

1 Make a loop round first two fingers of the left hand. Bring wire back up to thumb, tucking it under the thumb to hold in place.

2 Slide fingers out of the loop and hold wire with thumb and index finger. With your other hand, catch the working end of the wire and pull it through the loop.

3 Keep hold of the loop and bring the working wire and tail together. Pull on the working wire so that the loop becomes smaller, ready to put on your needle.

CASTING ON

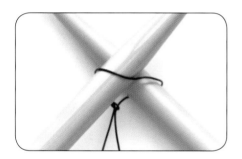  

1 Make a slip knot, and place on the left-hand needle. Insert the right-hand needle into the bottom of the stitch as shown.

2 Wrap the wire over the point of the right-hand needle then draw the loop through the first stitch.

3 Slide the stitch onto the left-hand needle. Continue until you have the required number of stitches.

KNIT STITCH

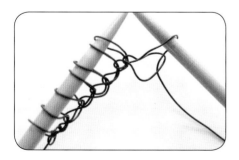 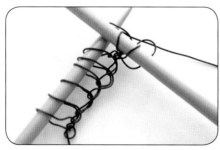 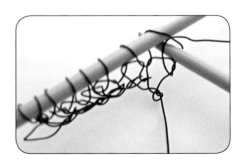

1 Cast on the required number of stitches and hold the needle in the left hand. Insert the right-hand needle into the first stitch. Wrap the wire over the needle from left to right and draw the loop through.

2 This time, instead of putting the loop back onto the left-hand needle, leave it on the right and slide the loop off the left-hand needle. Continue in this way with the rest of the stitches.

3 When all the loops are on the right-hand needle, put it into your left hand and start the process again.

BEADING IN KNITTING

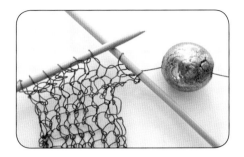

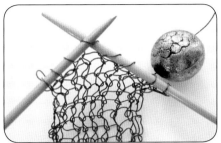

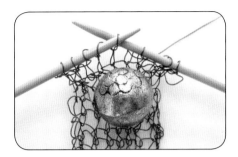

1 Work until you are ready to place a bead and then bring a bead up the wire. This example uses eight stitches.

2 Beading row 1: Knit 2, Slip 4. Knit 1 stitch with the bead, to place it in position, then Knit 1.

3 Beading row 2: Knit 2, Knit 4 into the back of the stitch (this is easier than trying to knit into the front of the stitch). Knit 2.

BEADING ACROSS A ROW

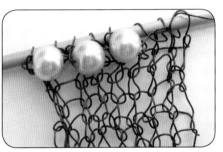

1 Bring a bead up the wire ready to place in your work. Knit the first stitch, and then place the bead.

2 Judge whether you can bead on every stitch or on alternate stitches; this depends on the size of the bead. Here the beads are placed on alternate stitches.

3 Give the beads enough space to sit well on your work. Always bead on the same side of the work—the one that faces away from you when knitting or crocheting.

BINDING OFF

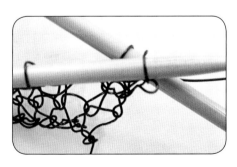

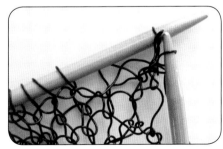

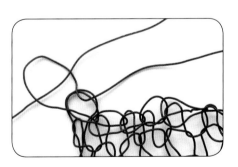

1 Knit the required length and then the first 2 stitches of next row. Insert left-hand needle into first stitch on right-hand needle.

2 Pass first stitch over the second stitch and drop it off the needle, leaving 1 stitch remaining. Knit 1 stitch from the left-hand needle, and repeat the process for the required number of stitches.

3 When only 1 stitch remains on the right-hand needle, cut the working end of the wire to about 4in (10cm). Pass the wire through the remaining stitch, pulling it gently to reduce its size.

Crochet techniques

CROCHET CHAIN STITCH

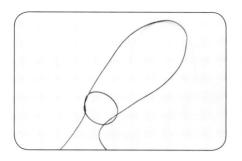

1 Make a slip knot (see page 40 for instructions).

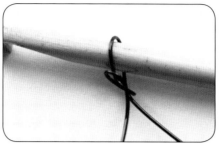

2 Insert the hook into the loop and tighten slightly.

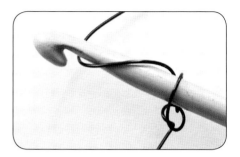

3 Holding the hook between the thumb and the index finger, and the tail in the left hand, pass the working wire over the top of the hook and under, forming a loop.

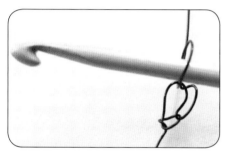

4 With the head of the hook turned to the left, pass it through the loop on the hook, catching the loop formed as you go.

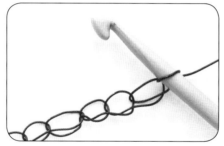

5 Repeat from step 3, keeping even tension on the wire. To finish off your work, pass the working end of the wire through the final loop of your work, and pull gently.

TECHNIQUE TIP...
The best way to get good results with crochet is to try to keep your tension even; do not be tempted to pull the loops tightly as you work them. If you haven't done crochet before it is worth working a few chains with some scrap wire before you start a project.

SLIP STITCH OR SINGLE CROCHET

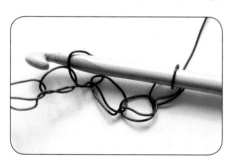

1 Work as for chain stitch but before passing the working wire over the hook, insert the hook into the work. This puts a second loop on the hook.

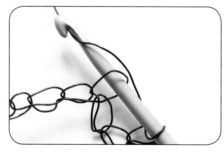

2 Pass the wire over the end of the hook, and draw the hook through both loops on the hook.

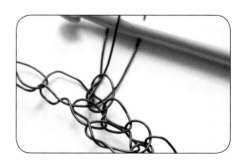

3 Repeat, taking care not to pull the work too tightly. Finish by passing the working wire through the final loop.

DOUBLE CROCHET (UK TREBLE CROCHET)

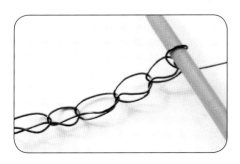

1 Start with a loop on the hook. Pass the wire over the hook.

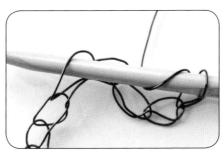

2 Insert the hook into the work (there will be three loops on the hook).

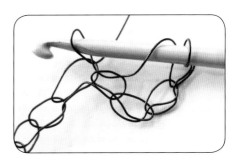

3 Pass the wire over the hook again and draw it through the first loop on the crochet hook (three loops on hook).

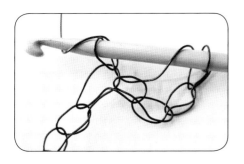

4 Pass the wire over the hook and draw it through the first two loops on the hook (two loops on hook).

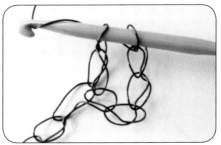

5 Pass the wire over the hook and draw it through the remaining two loops.

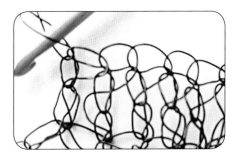

6 Continue for the required number of stitches, then finish off by passing the working wire through the final loop.

BEADING IN CROCHET

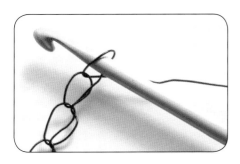

1 Thread the required number of beads onto the wire and work several chains.

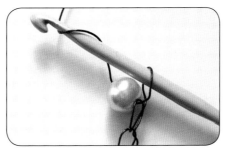

2 Place a bead into the desired position, then pass the wire over the hook and draw it through the loop.

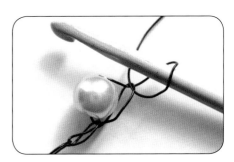

3 Continue with chain stitch; the bead should sit in the same position on the work. Continue placing beads where you require. Try to keep the tension even and the stitches a regular size.

How to French Knit

1 Make a slip knot (see page 40), leaving a long tail of wire. Put the loop over one of the bobbin pins, keeping it fairly loose.

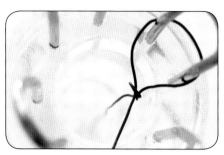

2 Pass the wire tail down the center of the bobbin. Working clockwise, take the wire across to the far edge of the next pin, around the back and then to the front, forming a loop of wire around the pin.

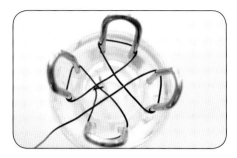

3 Continue round the next pins until you are back at the slip knot pin. Work a loop around this pin too.

4 Using a metal point, lift the bottom stitch over the top one.

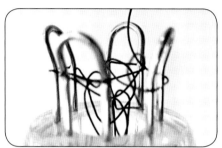

5 Continue in a clockwise direction. After each stitch, give a gentle tug on the wire at the bottom of the bobbin. To finish off, carefully slide the four loops off the pins.

6 Pass working end of the wire through the loops. Pull the working end gently, but firmly, to gather the ends together neatly.

How to Plait

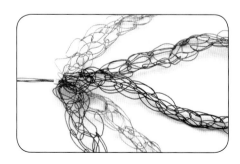

1 Secure five strands together at the end and fix to a secure base. (Use a spare wire to attach to a drawer handle or similar.) Spread the strands out.

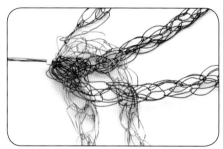

2 Cross the outside right strand over the two strands to its left so it goes to the middle. Cross the left strand over the two strands to its right, so it goes to the middle.

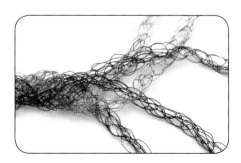

3 Repeat for the length of the strands. The work can be squeezed and teased into shape when you have finished, and before any fastenings are attached.

Finishing Off

ATTACHING FASTENINGS

You can buy many different types of fastening so choose one that is appropriate to the work. A chunky necklace needs to be matched with a fairly chunky fastening. I prefer fastenings to be discreet; however, you might like to make a statement and use something big and bold at the front of the necklace. Bracelets often have a ring-and-bar type of fastening, for ease of use.

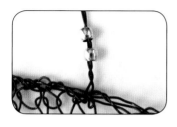

1 Feed two crimp beads onto the finishing wire.

2 Check that the ring is closed on the fastening. Squeeze gently with pliers to secure.

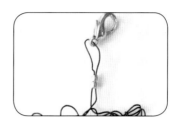

3 Pass the finishing wires through the loop and through both crimp beads.

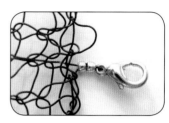

4 Gently pull the wire tails to close the wire loop.

5 Squeeze the crimp beads with pliers and snip off the wire ends.

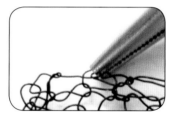

6 Check that the wire ends are not sticking out. Then, if necessary, bend them back on themselves with the pliers.

7 Repeat for the other half of the fastening. Here, you can see a barrel-type fastening.

MAKING A FASTENING LOOP

Sometimes it is useful to make your own loops for fastening.

1 Twist the finishing wire and feed two crimp beads onto it.

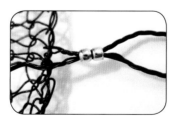

2 Push the twisted wire back down the crimp beads.

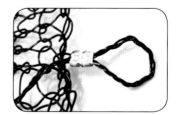

3 Adjust the size and squeeze the crimp beads with pliers to secure in place.

4 Finish off the tail.

MAKING BRACELETS AND EARRINGS

Bracelets

To make a bracelet to match the necklaces in this book, simply make a shorter version. Measure round your wrist, remembering that if it is too tight the bracelet will be difficult to fasten. Some bracelets will not require a fastening at all, and can simply be wrapped around the wrist a few times.

Fastenings for bracelets

Larger round or lobster fastenings can be used for bracelets. Alternatively, you can use a ring-and-bar fastening—if using this type of fastener, the bracelet will need to be shorter. A twist fastening is suitable only for lighter-weight bracelets. Magnetic clasps are best avoided as you can easily lose your bracelet.

Earrings

Earrings can be made in the same way as the necklace, but shorter. Their size will depend on your personal taste and the weight of earrings you prefer.

For pierced ears, two types of finding are available: a post type or a fish-hook style. Don't forget the backs for the post type, which are often sold separately. If you prefer clip-on earrings, be aware that some are only suitable for sticking a stone on and don't have a loop to attach the earring.

ATTACHING A FASTENING TO AN EARRING

1 Feed two crimp beads onto the finishing wire.

2 Ensure that the earring loop is fully closed.

3 Pass the finishing wire through the loop and the two crimp beads.

4 Gently pull the finishing wire so that the crimp beads are next to the earring.

5 Crimp and cut off the wire as close as possible to the crimps. Make sure there are no ends sticking out.

Troubleshooting

SNAPPED WIRE IN THE MIDDLE OF THE WORK

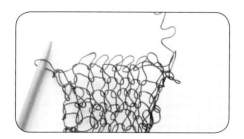

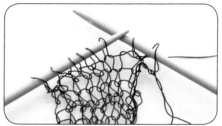

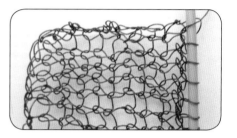

1 Undo a little of the work to give you a "tail" to work with.

2 Take a matching reel of wire and thread any beads from the old reel onto the new reel. Leave another tail of wire before restarting your work with the new reel. Twist the two tails together and continue.

3 Complete the work. Then return to the two tails and weave them into the necklace. Don't weave them together as this can make the work bulky. The idea is to disguise the ends so they don't show.

SNAPPED WIRE AT THE END OF THE WORK

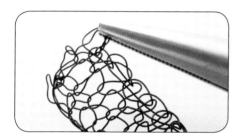

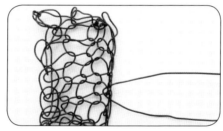

1 Hide broken wire by folding it around another wire and squeezing with pliers.

2 Use a separate piece of wire to attach the fastenings. The wire should be double thickness for this.

HIDING ENDS

There are three basic methods for hiding ends. Choose the most appropriate method, remembering to check that there are no uncomfortable wires sticking out.

1 Weave the ends into the work. Weave in opposite directions so the work doesn't become too bulky. Cut and crimp the ends into the work.

2 Tuck the ends inside beads. Feed them through the crimp beads and cut off as close to the crimps as possible.

TIPS...

Wire unraveling off the reel
Put the reel inside a plastic zipped bag and seal, apart from a small gap through which to feed the wire.

First stitch of French knitting proving difficult
Make the slip loop looser, and you will find that it passes over the hook of the bobbin much more easily.

Finishing off French knitting
It can be difficult to feed the wire through the bobbin loops while they are on the bobbin. Slide them off and push a cable needle through the loops to gather together. Feed through the working wire. Pull, tightening the loops.

Conversions

WIRE CONVERSION CHARTS

Wire can be measured either by gauge or diameter. These charts show the approximate metric conversion of the American Wire Gauge (AWG) and the Standard Wire Gauge (SWG).

American Wire Gauge	Equivalent in mm (AWG)
33	0.18
32	0.20
31	0.22
30	0.25
29	0.29
28	0.32
27	0.36
26	0.40
25	0.45
24	0.51
23	0.57
22	0.64
21	0.72
20	0.81
19	0.91
18	1.02

Standard Wire Gauge	Equivalent in mm (SWG)
38	0.15
37	0.17
36	0.19/0.20
35	0.21
34	0.23
33	0.25
32	0.27
31	0.29
30	0.30/0.31
29	0.34
28	0.37
27	0.41
26	0.45
25	0.5
24	0.59
23	0.61
22	0.71
21	0.81
20	0.91
19	1.01
18	1.21

KNITTING AND CROCHET CHARTS

KNITTING NEEDLE SIZES

Metric (mm)	US	UK
2	0	14
2.25	1	13
2.75	2	12
3	–	11
3.25	3	10
3.5	4	–
3.75	5	9
4	6	8
4.5	7	7
5	8	6
5.5	9	5
6	10	4
6.5	10.5	3
7	–	2
7.5	–	1
8	11	0
9	13	00
10	15	000

CROCHET HOOK SIZES

Metric (mm)	US	UK
10	P-15	000
9	N-13	00
8	L-11	0
7	K-10	1/22
6.5	10 1/4	3
6	J-10	4
5.5	I-9	5
5	H-8	6
4.5	7	7
4	G-6	8
3.75	F-5	9
3.5	E-4	9
3.25	D-3	10
2.75	C-2	12
2.25	B-1	13
2	B-0	14

UK/US CROCHET TERMS

UK	US
Double crochet	Single crochet
Half treble	Half double crochet
Treble	Double crochet
Cast off	Bind off